EXPLORER

PLANTS!

By **Nick Forshaw** & **William Exley**

What on Earth Books

What on Earth Publishing Ltd., The Black Barn, Wickhurst Farm, Tonbridge, Kent TN11 8PS, United Kingdom

First published in 2019.

Produced with the assistance of experts at the Natural History Museum, London, UK.

Written by Nick Forshaw.
Illustrated by William Exley.
Designed by Andy Forshaw and Assunção Sampayo.
Edited by Patrick Skipworth.

BISAC:
JNF037030: Juvenile Nonfiction / Science & Nature / Flowers & Plants

Library of Congress Cataloging-in-Publication Data available upon request

ISBN: 978-93-5954-642-1

Published and Distributed in India by
Scholastic India Pvt. Ltd.

This Reprint Edition: August, 2024

Printed in India

CONTENTS

MISSION INSTRUCTIONS

AGENT ASSIGNED: Agent Osprey

YOUR MISSION: Calling Agent Osprey! You must once again venture into the unknown. Explorer HQ needs a report on plants ASAP! Go out and examine every flower and tree you can see.

CLASSIFIED

AGENT OSPREY

Map Archives

I'm Ada Osprey, Senior Librarian of the Eagle-Eyed Explorer Club. Years ago, the club recruited me as one of its special agents—codename Agent Osprey.
Most days you'll find me in the basement of the library, organizing the atlases. But I always keep my rucksack at the ready, in case the club needs me for one of its urgent missions. I never know when to expect a call.

STAFF ROOM ←
LIBRARY ←
PLANTS! →
Mission Checklist
1x Explorer Field Notebook
1x Magnifying Glass
1x Binoculars
1x Agent Issue Flashlight
1x Portable Time Machine
1x Sandwich (peanut butter)
My latest mission is not only top secret, but very dangerous, so keep it hush-hush. The club has ordered me to file a report on the entire history of plants as soon as possible. It looks like I'll need to go back millions of years in time.

EXPLORATIONS
ON EARTH HAPPENED?
SUPERASER PRO
EXPLORER
PLANTS!
I'll need to fill out a Journal to keep track of my discoveries. I'm also drawing up a Timeline to show the life story of plants, from the ancient seas to the present day.

No time to waste. Are you feeling brave? Let's go!

1. WHAT ARE PLANTS?

"Over millions of years, plants have evolved from tiny strands floating in the ocean into some of the most gigantic living things in the world. An oak tree or a fern bush, a cactus or a sunflower, green fields covered with grass or jungles thick with vines—plants grow in every environment on planet Earth. Plants are essential to how life on Earth works, providing food, energy, even the oxygen we breathe. But how did all this start? Where did plants begin?"

Before the Plants

Three billion years ago, as the sun shone over the seas, early life-forms were flourishing underwater. These ancient organisms were "cyanobacteria." The cyanobacteria were tiny, made up of one single cell. In an empty ocean with little else to feed on, they had discovered a unique way to stay alive. They absorbed the light from the sun to create the energy to survive. This miraculous way of making energy is called "photosynthesis." It's the secret to how all plants survive today.

As time passed, the cyanobacteria began to combine with other organisms. The other organisms relied on the energy the cyanobacteria created. Soon, these organisms began to develop into a soggy seaweed called "algae." The cyanobacteria remained inside the algae's cells, but in the form of a small green capsule called a "chloroplast." The chloroplasts absorbed the sunlight and used photosynthesis to create energy. The energy gave the algae strength to grow. Little by little, over millions and millions of years, new kinds of algae began to form, which were stronger and more solid. Photosynthesis continued to be the secret to their survival. As we will discover, these algae are the ancient ancestors of all the different kinds of plants growing on Earth today.

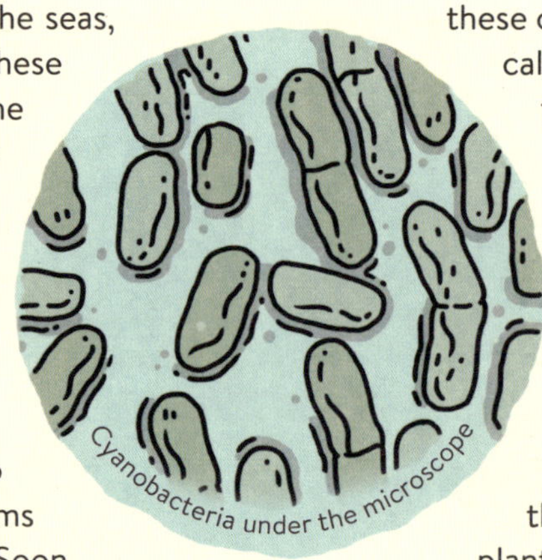
Cyanobacteria under the microscope

Adapting to New Surroundings

Evolution is a process of change, where, over time, organisms' bodies adapt to their environments. These changes help them to survive. New generations may come into the world with bodies that differ slightly from their parents', but these differences may give them a better chance of survival. Such changes are called "adaptations."

The ancient cyanobacteria evolved with an adaptation that enabled them to make energy from sunlight. Then other living things absorbed the cyanobacteria, and evolved into kinds of algae. The algae still relied on the energy the cyanobacteria provided. But over millions of years, the ancient algae changed too. Some kinds of algae eventually evolved into plants that we would recognize today. On sunny tropical shores, plants such as palms evolved with huge leaves. They could absorb lots of sunlight to generate energy. In deserts with little rain, cactus plants evolved with sturdy bodies. They could store essential water which is otherwise in short supply.

Adaptations help plants survive in different environments

PLANT PROFILE: OAK

EXPLORER NOTES: *Different species can have slightly different characteristics*

Getting Organized

To see the connections between living things, scientists organize plants and animals into different groups. The members of each group all share similar characteristics. Scientists place all the plants that produce flowers into one of these groups. They call the flowering plants group the "angiosperms." And they place all the oak trees into a smaller group called "*Quercus*." Even within a group, there can be further differences as well. To tell the different oak trees apart, scientists divide the groups into "species." The "turkey" oak (*Quercus cerris*) is a species of oak tree that grows in the United States. The "English" oak (*Quercus robur*) is a species of oak tree that grows in England. Its leaves are a different shape from those of the turkey oak. Their differences reflect how these species have evolved in ways that help them survive in their own environments.

"Turn the page to discover more about different types of plants!"

What shapes and sizes are plants?

Some plants grow close to the ground, others reach right up to the sky. North American redwood trees are gigantic. They are some of the largest organisms alive. They can grow to 360 feet tall, with rust-colored trunks and needle-like leaves. But down on the forest floor, mosses spill out at ground level. They grow on every bump and crevice. Their compact green leaves have a springy texture that's soft to touch.

How do new plants grow?

Reproduction is an essential part of a plant's life. Some plants let out "spores," delicate grains from which new plants can grow. Other plants such as magnolia rely on their flowers to produce their offspring. The flowers attract insects and other animals. These visitors to the plant accidentally pick up the pollen on the flowers' stamens – special structures hidden between the petals. As they travel on their way, the creatures bring the pollen to the flowers of other plants. When pollen from one plant mixes with the egg cells of another, the egg cells are ready to become seeds from which new plants will grow.

How have plants adapted to new environments?

With broad leaves or slim stems, thick trunks or sharp thorns, plants develop in many different forms. Each of these adaptations can help them survive in their environments. In dense forests, trees grow to great heights to reach the sunlight. In fields where plant-eating animals roam, thistles have prickly spines that stop them being eaten. Some trees have evolved in ways that are so successful they can live for a very long time. In North America, there are bristlecone pines that first sprouted thousands of years ago. Even today, they are still growing healthy and strong.

2. PLANT ORIGINS

COOKSONIA

"In the Devonian period, 400 million years ago, algae continued to slosh around in the seas and lakes. Some algae species had developed into stronger forms. Stoneworts, ancient algae that still exist today, grew with thin lace-like branches. But outside of the water, something new was happening. For the first time, plants began to grow on dry land. Their bodies had changed almost entirely, adapting in new ways to survive in a new world."

New Arrivals

Spread out among the sand and gravel on dry land, nestling in between rocky crags, slim green organisms were sprouting everywhere. These new organisms were relatives of the algae that had flourished underwater. On every surface, these curious slender tubes grew out of the earth and pointed toward the sun.

Plants such as *Cooksonia* grew in great numbers all over the terrain. It was one of the first land-based plants. Like its underwater ancestors, it produced energy from the sun by photosynthesis. *Cooksonia* had a tube-like body with simple branches. Each branch ended in a sack which released spores into the air. Wherever the spores landed, a new plant could grow, helping its species to thrive. *Cooksonia* had adapted to withstand the challenges of dry land. A curled stem helped it hook solidly into the ground. Water flowing through its body kept it upright and stable.

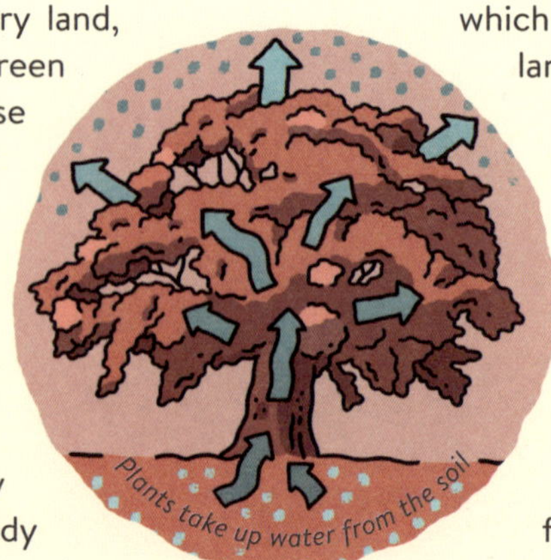

Other organisms were evolving alongside—and even inside—*Cooksonia*, too. Microscopic fungi growing within its body absorbed some of the energy the plant produced. At the same time, *Cooksonia* benefited from the nutrients the fungi sucked up from the soil. Fungi aren't plants, but the two life-forms worked together to survive.

Living on Dry Land

To survive outside lakes and rivers, the new plants needed to find water on dry land. *Cooksonia*'s stem sucked up water from the soil in which it grew. The water flow helped to keep the plant upright. But *Calamophyton*, another early plant, had evolved with an even more ingenious method of locating a water supply. This species was one of the first to grow roots. These drilled down into the earth and took up water and nutrients from the soil.

Most plants today rely on their roots for water. Modern fig trees can grow up to heights of 33 feet, but underground, their roots reach down to much greater depths. They can burrow through the earth for 395 feet. The tangled mass of roots holds the tree securely in place and they suck up water from deep down to feed the tree.

The Search for Sunlight

Early plants relied on their slim stems alone to catch the sun's light. Some species however, began to evolve with features that helped them catch even more sunshine. *Calamophyton* had thin, fuzzy bristles at its head. Every one of these bristles absorbed extra light from the sun. The bristles were early forms of leaves. They helped the plant to absorb as much sunshine as possible.

As new plant species began to evolve, there was more competition to absorb the most light. This meant some species evolved with differently shaped leaves, battling it out in their habitat to soak up the sun. Plants' leaves can be flat and round, thin and pointed, rough and curled, or jagged and sharp. Each shape reveals how the plant has evolved in its own way to absorb as much sunlight as possible in its environment.

"Turn the page to discover more about the first plants!"

PLANT PROFILE: *CALAMOPHYTON*

EXPLORER NOTES: *This ancient plant had lots of remarkable adaptations*

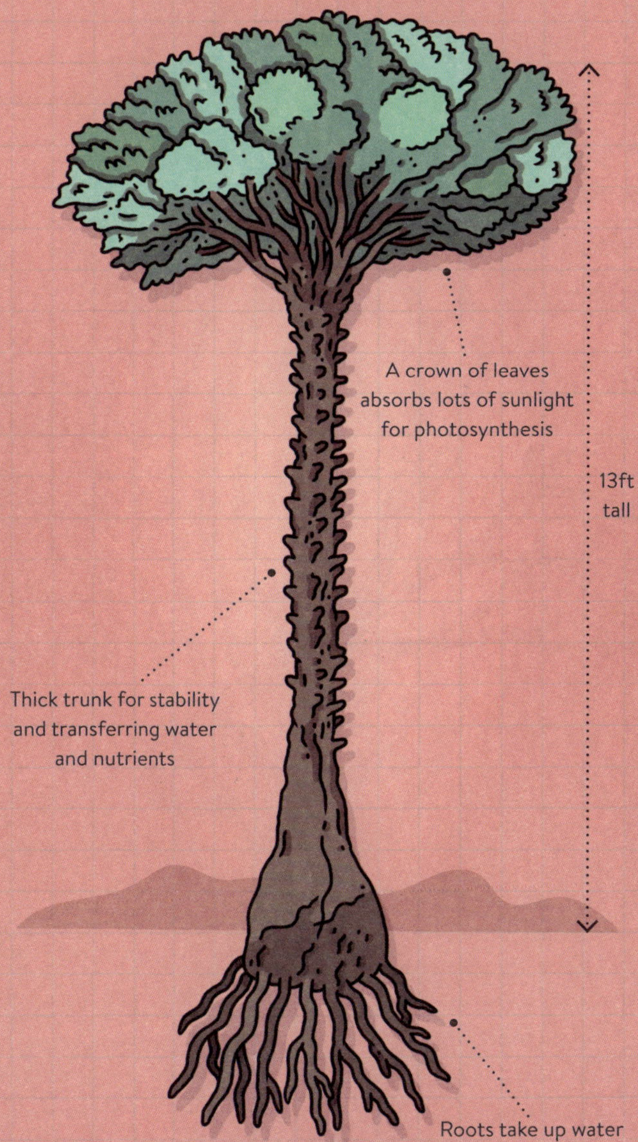

What were the first plants?

The first plants developed with incredible adaptations which helped them survive. Even though they looked as if they came from outer space, their features can still be seen on plants today. Here are my notes on some of these early arrivals to dry land.

HORNEOPHYTON ⋮ HEIGHT – 8in.

EXPLORER NOTES: *Simple plant with several branches*

One of the earliest plants to grow on land. It sprouted all over the gritty terrain of the time, with a compact, turnip-like body buried solidly in the earth. It sucked up water from the surrounding soil through its slim stem. The water helped to keep the plant upright and stable.

TIMELINE DATE *410 million years ago*

ASTEROXYLON ⋮ HEIGHT – 20in.

EXPLORER NOTES: *Covered in scale-like leaves*

One of the first plant species to evolve with leaves. The leaves grew tightly together all along its long green stem, forming a mesh of spiky plates. Across these compact pointy scales were many tiny holes. These holes released oxygen into the air as the plant photosynthesized.

TIMELINE DATE *410 million years ago*

DREPANOPHYCUS ⋮ HEIGHT – 3ft

EXPLORER NOTES: *Covered in spiny, needle-like leaves*

Leaning out over the dust, *Drepanophycus* grew to around 3 feet tall. This was much larger than many other plant species at the time. Its long body bristled with thin spiky leaves that grew along its stem from top to bottom. *Drepanophycus* was one of the first plants to have evolved with "veins" inside its small leaves. These tubes transported nutrients and fluids essential for growth.

TIMELINE DATE *400 million years ago*

PSILOPHYTON | HEIGHT – 3ft

EXPLORER NOTES: *Grew in great numbers along marshes and swamps*

Lining the waterways that crisscrossed the terrain, *Psilophyton* grew in masses over wetland environments. It could be found sprouting all around marshlands and shallow swamps. Simple branching stems found on plants such as these would develop into the first leaves.

TIMELINE DATE *390 million years ago*

RHACOPHYTON | HEIGHT – 5ft

EXPLORER NOTES: *Tiny branches where photosynthesis took place*

Rhacophyton grew in dense, thick throngs around swamps and marshlands. Its thin green, leaf-like branches nudged against each other as they absorbed the sunlight. It grew in great numbers all over its soggy habitat—it was one of the most successful plant species to have evolved in this period.

TIMELINE DATE *385 million years ago*

ARCHEOPTERIS | HEIGHT – 33ft

EXPLORER NOTES: *Early tree grew to great heights*

Many small plants were thriving in this prehistoric environment. But one species had evolved to grow taller than the rest. Most other plants grew to barely more than 3 feet in height. But *Archeopteris* grew to over 33 feet tall. It was one of the first true trees, with a tough skin of bark protecting its trunk. Large leaves much like those of later plants, such as conifers, flopped down from its branches. But it still reproduced with spores, like older plants. This unusual combination is not found anywhere today.

TIMELINE DATE *370 million years ago*

3. PLANT PLANET

CARBONIFEROUS FOREST

"The Carboniferous environment, around 360–300 million years ago, was damp and humid. The land was wet with swamps and marshes. Insects buzzed and reptiles scampered around. Plants thrived in these wet conditions and grew all over the environment. The oxygen the plants released as they photosynthesized altered the atmosphere. This changing environment began to influence the growth of new kinds of animals. The sun shone down on a lush new planet, a world that plants had created."

The Jungles of the Carboniferous

Some of the most common Carboniferous plants were ferns, plants with delicate triangular leaves. Others were seed ferns, a unique group which no longer survives today. Their bushy bunches covered the forest glades. Horsetail plants rose up from the undergrowth. These slim plants had fuzzy leaves sprouting from their tall stems. Thick forests of *Lepidodendron* spread out over the land. These early trees could grow 130 feet high. They formed dense jungles around the swamps. Their trunks were covered by a puzzle of diamond shapes, which were the scars their gigantic leaves left behind when they fell off.

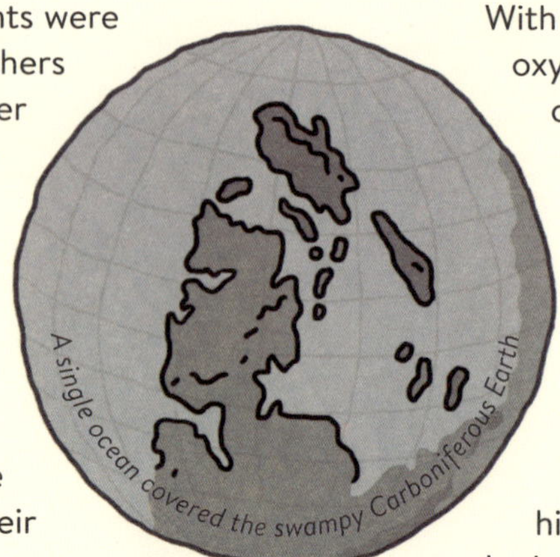

A single ocean covered the swampy Carboniferous Earth

With so many plants photosynthesizing together, oxygen levels rose. This began to affect the way other living creatures grew. Zipping in between the plant stems were gigantic flying insects. Their massive sizes were supported by the great quantities of oxygen being released into the atmosphere. But sometimes all this oxygen could be dangerous. Fires need oxygen to burn, and huge forests may have often caught light and burned to the ground. Left behind were ghostly gray and blackened hillsides, silent traces of the vibrant plant life that had once lived there.

Fern leaves or "fronds" grow curled up before unfurling

A Forest of Ferns

Ferns are delicate plants that grow best when the air is moist and humid. In such warm and damp conditions, fern plants began to flourish. Some ferns only grew to less than ½ inch tall. Others like "tree ferns" reached up to 33 feet in height. Their riffled leaves branched out from a central "frond." This way the leaves could catch the most sunlight for photosynthesis. From the underside of their leaves, they released hundreds of thousands of "spores" into the air. The spores could grow up into new fern plants when they hit the right patch of ground.

Fossilized Plants

How did the Carboniferous get its name? The word "Carboniferous" refers to carbon—the main ingredient in coal. Humans have been digging this black rock out of the ground for thousands of years. Throughout history they have burned it to produce energy. But coal is not simply another rock—it comes from the ancient remains of dead plants. Over millions of years the plant remains have been squashed down and dried out by the environment. The energy these dead plants can release is incredibly powerful. It can power steam engines and factories. During the Industrial Revolution in the eighteenth and nineteenth centuries, coal-powered machines changed the way society worked. Coal continues to provide energy in modern times. But burning coal produces pollution and damages the environment. The plants and animals alive today are at risk from the way humans burn the remains of plants from the past.

CARBONIFEROUS COAL

EXPLORER NOTES: *Coal is formed from plants and burned by humans for energy*

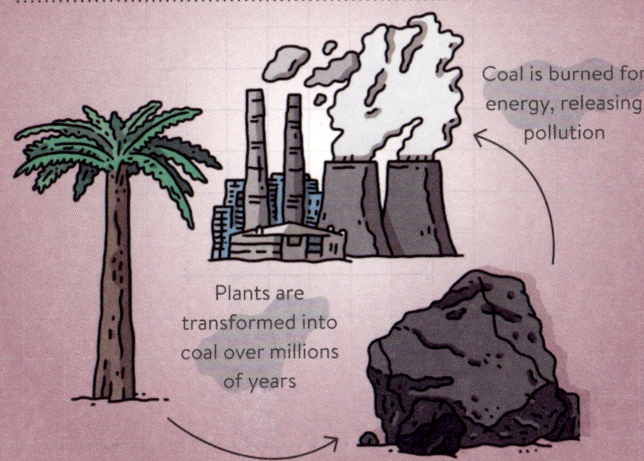

"Turn the page to discover the different environments plants live in today!"

Forest

All across the northern hemisphere, great forests thick with trees survive through the changing seasons. In fall and winter, the fragile leaves of many trees can struggle to survive the harsh conditions. So these trees lose their leaves instead, preserving their nutrients and water. In the spring, the leaves grow back, ready to provide energy from the sun.

Jungle

There is nowhere on Earth where more kinds of organisms live side by side than in the jungle. Plants are at the center of jungle life. Gigantic trees, hanging vines, tangled roots, low-growing shrubs, delicate ferns—without plants, there would be no jungle at all! Jungle plants thrive in hot and rainy climates. They spread out around long rivers which form in these damp environments. As the plants photosynthesize, they release great quantities of oxygen into the air.

Desert

Plants can thrive even in the hot, dry environment of the desert. Some desert plants have thick stems that help them survive. Cactus plants keep essential water in their fleshy bodies. Their sharp needles protect them against bites from thirsty animals. In season, cactuses can produce flowers and fruit. The fruits' bright colors attract animals' attention, which can help the plants disperse their seeds after the fruit is eaten.

Savanna

The savanna is home to many different plant species. Each has evolved with its own way of combating the hot conditions. Many different kinds of grasses survive even in the dry environment. Short-trunked trees grow with roots that spread out for great distances underground to find water. In such dry conditions, fire is a constant threat. A lightning storm may cause the vegetation to catch light, risking bush fires that can last for weeks.

4. SURVIVAL STRATEGIES

CONIFERS

"In the Permian period, 300–250 million years ago, plants grew all over the land and great green forests spread out far and wide. Conifers and tree ferns flourished in dense clusters, palm-like cycads and ginkgo trees sprouted among marshes and swamps. The new plants' leaves helped them photosynthesize, their roots helped them draw water, and their seeds helped them reproduce. But how did they spread so successfully in the first place? Where do new plants come from? How do new plants grow?"

The Hidden Power of Seeds

Most plants today grow from seeds, which develop into shoots that sprout from the soil. Early plants reproduced in a more basic way. They simply let out "spores" into the air, which would be carried around their habitat by the wind. Spores are delicate clusters of cells. If a spore lands on healthy ground, it begins to grow into a new plant. Ferns protect their spores beneath their leaves. When caught in a breeze, the spores are carried out to new territory. There they can start to grow into the next generation of ferns.

Without a strong coating however, spores can be vulnerable. As plants evolved, they developed stronger means of protection. Tall seed ferns were the first plants to protect their spores inside a special casing. These new kinds of spores were the very first seeds! Seeds have thick outer layers that protect the cells inside from tough environments. The outer layers stop them from drying out in the air. Seeds frequently contain extra energy and water supplies too. This helps the seed develop into a plant straight away. Seed ferns are no longer around—they were probably wiped out with the dinosaurs at the end of the Cretaceous period. But almost all the different kinds of plants that grow today flourish thanks to seeds.

Huge forests of conifers cover cold regions today

Conifers

Conifer trees were some of the most successful plants growing in the Permian period. They spread out all over the landscape in great green forests. Other plants and animals lived in these forests too. Conifers stored their seeds in cones at the end of their branches, just like they do today. They were some of the first plants to protect their seeds in this way. As the wind blows through the conifers, it can carry the seeds with it. Or sometimes the seeds get spread across the ground when the cone opens or falls from the tree. On ground level, the seeds are ready to grow into new conifer trees. While over time other plants became more widespread, conifers still grow in great numbers today. They can be found all across snowy forests.

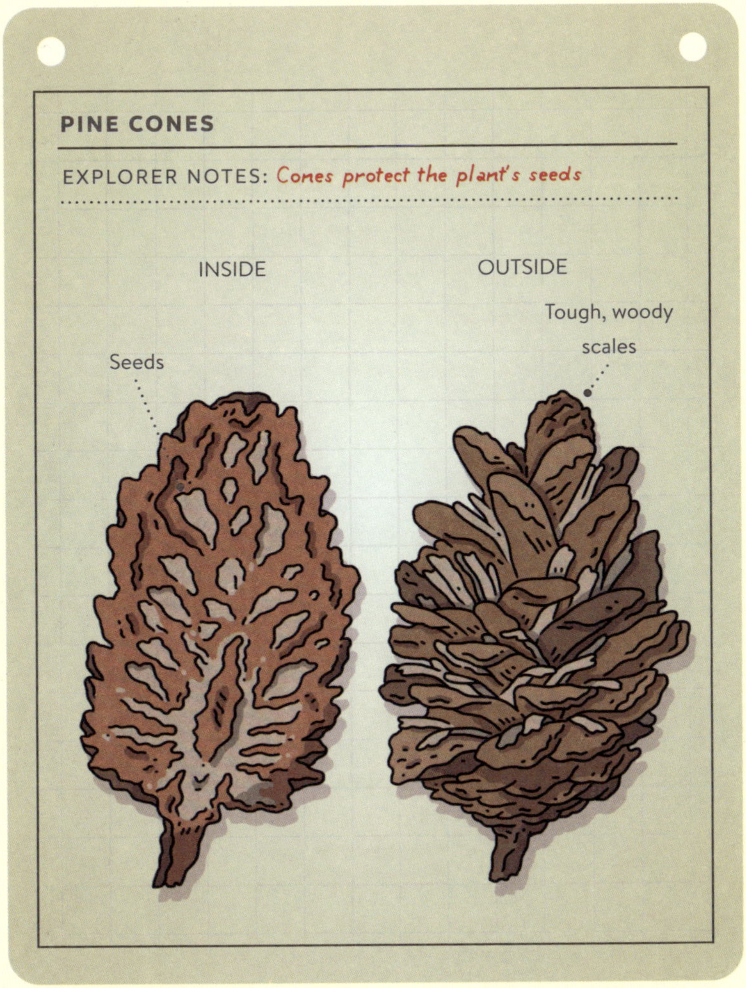

Cycads were common food for plant-eating dinosaurs

Cycads

Cycads are plants with fuzzy trunks and long, riffling green leaves that sprout out from the top. They first began to grow in the Permian period, over 270 million years ago. By the arrival of the dinosaurs in the Triassic period, they were found all across the globe. Cycads would have been a regular part of a plant-eating dinosaur's diet. They were a favorite food of gigantic *Diplodocus* and armored *Stegosaurus*.

Cycads still survive today. Like many plants, certain cycads need insects to help them reproduce. Some species can raise their temperatures, inviting insects to nestle in their warm cones. Then they drop their temperatures back down again. This sends the insects on their way. The insects may have unknowingly picked up the cycad's pollen on their visit. They bring this pollen to new cycads as they journey from plant to plant. This helps the cycads reproduce.

"Turn the page to discover the clever strategies plants use to survive!"

What special strategies do plants use to stay alive?

On our planet, more creatures eat plants than eat meat. To avoid becoming a plant-eating animal's next meal, plants have developed with adaptations that help them survive. Some use sharp spines, others use deadly poison. Some rely on their size to avoid being devoured. But there is always an exception to the rule. Some plants may actually want animals to eat them, to insure the growth of the next generation. Here are my notes on some of the survival tricks plants use to avoid getting chomped up . . .

POISON | *STRYCHNOS*

EXPLORER NOTES: *Deadly toxins stop hungry animals in their tracks*

Strychnos plants have a secret way to avoid being eaten up. Although you cannot tell from the outside, they contain a deadly poison in their bark and leaves. A single bite can be fatal for a plant-eating animal. Some creatures are not affected by the plant's poison however, and enjoy eating its fruit.

HEIGHT | *ARAUCARIOXYLON*

EXPLORER NOTES: *Size can be one of the best defenses against plant-eaters*

Growing tall helps plants survive. Plant-eating animals can't reach their leaves, which grow up high to catch more sun. 200 million years ago, giant plant-eating dinosaurs tried to eat plants of all sizes. But *Araucarioxylon*'s 200-foot height meant its leaves were often out of reach. It had a woody trunk, which was too tough for plant-eaters to feed on. Modern creatures such as giraffes or elephants can reach high-up leaves, but growing tall still helps trees survive today.

HEAT | CHILI PEPPER

EXPLORER NOTES: *A spicy kick keeps most animals away*

Many plants rely on animals to eat their fruits and the seeds contained inside. As the animals move around their habitat, they pass the seeds out in their droppings. This helps plants spread their seeds over greater distances. The seeds grow into new plants. Chili plants have developed a way to spread their seeds as far as possible. Chilies may be too spicy for most animals, but not birds. They happily feed on chili peppers. The birds carry the chili seeds out far and wide, whether hunting, nest-building, or even migrating. They take the seeds to new ground where they can grow into new plants.

THORNS | ROSE

EXPLORER NOTES: *Sharp spines keep grazers at bay*

Some plants use spiky armor to defend themselves against hungry creatures. Chunky cactuses have sharp spikes on their bulky bodies, to pierce any animal trying to take a bite. Roses are plants with prickly thorns on their stems. Their sweet and colorful flowers may attract insects. But their sharp spikes deter any plant-eaters trying to eat them up.

INSECT GUARDS | ANT-HOUSE PLANT

EXPLORER NOTES: *An army of ants protects this plant*

This lumpy plant has its own private army crawling around inside its stem. A colony of ants lives inside the ant plant's stem and protects it from predators. The ants scurry through the dozens of tunnels and chambers hidden inside. The ants protect the plant, but the plant protects them too by offering them a home.

MEAT-EATERS | VENUS FLYTRAP

EXPLORER NOTES: *Turns the tables on hungry animals*

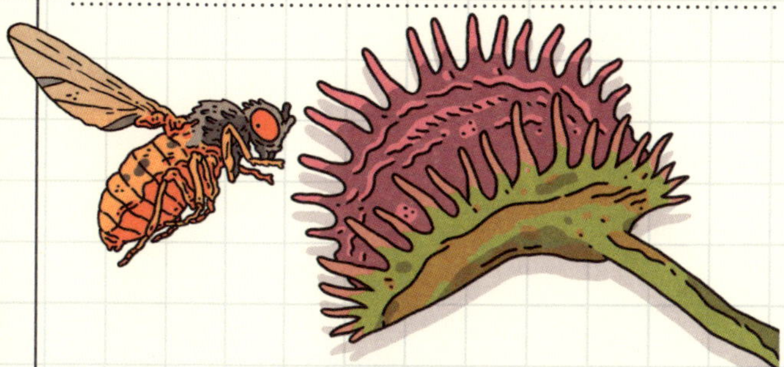

Many animals like to eat plants, but there are some plants that like to eat animals too! The Venus flytrap's leaves have developed in a way that makes them look like a green mouth, complete with spiky teeth and even a pink tongue. Curious insects venture in, attracted by a sweet syrup inside. But if they make too many movements, they set off the trap. In an instant, the plant's green "mouth" snaps shut. Stuck inside the trap, the plant slowly digests its insect prisoner over many days.

5. FRUITS AND FLOWERS

EAGLE-EYED · LIBRARY ·

FLOWERING PLANTS

"Seeds were not the only new development that helped plants successfully spread out across the Earth. In the Cretaceous period, 66–145 million years ago, at the edges of a watery marsh, a small green plant had begun to grow a soft flower. It may have been the first ever plant to evolve this way. Soon, many plants began to grow flowers. Today they are found in different colors, shapes, and smells. Flowers help plants thrive across the world."

The First Flowers

Flowering plants bloom all over the countryside. They grow in colorful meadows or woodland glades, by busy streams or in a green forests. Their flowers have vibrant colors and different shapes. In the jungle, delicate orchids hang between vines and creepers. On marshy ponds, white water lilies float peacefully. In a dark wood, cherry trees blossom with pink petals. Out in the desert, cactus flowers bloom at night. Flowers have helped plants spread out and thrive for millions of years. But what was the first flower?

One of the first plants to grow flowers was *Archefructus*. This water plant could be found in lakes 130 million years ago. Not long after, flowering plants began to spread all over the planet. New types of flowers of different shapes, color and sizes developed quickly too. So many different plant species developed flowers around the same time, that revolutionary biologist Charles Darwin called the puzzle of their appearance "the Great Mystery." Soon flowers flourished across the globe, becoming an essential part of every environment. Flowers have been such a revolutionary adapatation that today flowering plants are the most diverse and widespread group of plants.

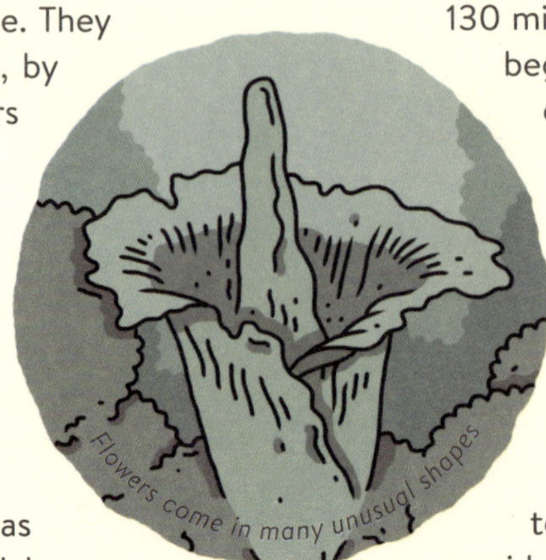

Flowers come in many unusual shapes

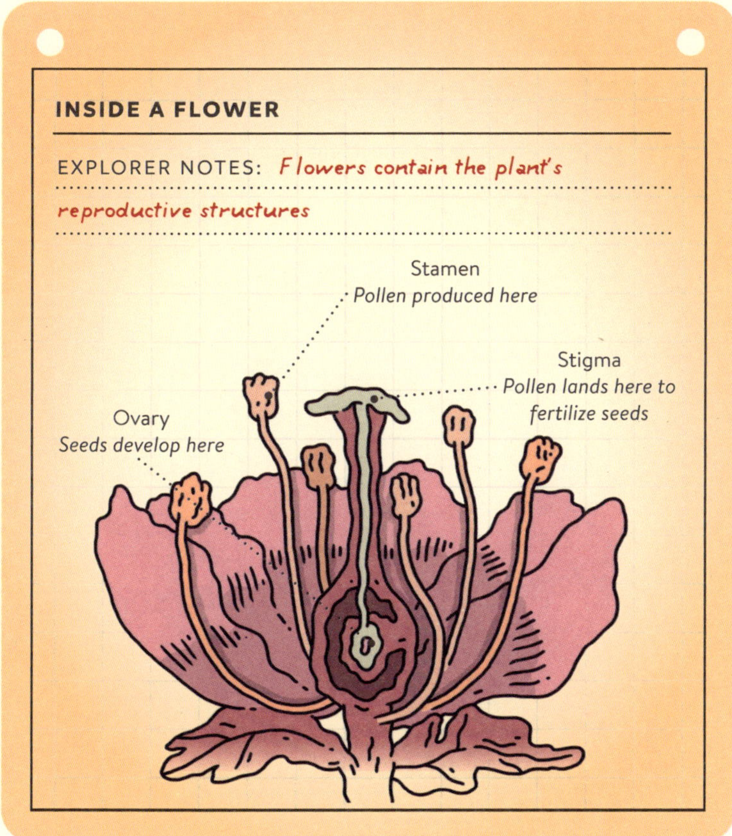

Petals and Pollen

Flowers are much more than colorful decorations. They are the parts of a plant where new seeds first develop. They continue to protect the seeds as they grow. Seeds start off as "ovules" in the female part of the flower, hidden between its petals. When the ovules are touched by a grain of pollen, they become fertilized and turn into seeds. Pollen comes from the long, thin male parts of a flower. But how does the pollen get to the egg cell in the first place? Although pollen can be carried on the wind, insects are the main way pollen is spread around. The insects are attracted by the flowers' bright colors and the sweet nectar they contain. As they explore inside, they pick up the pollen on their bodies. When they visit other flowers, the pollen may fall off. Then it travels to the new flower's ovules, helping them grow into seeds. This process seems simple, but flowers have helped plants flourish for millions of years.

From Flower to Fruit

When its seeds are ready, a part of the plant's flowers slowly turns into a fruit. The seeds are kept inside. A peach or a plum, a pear or a pineapple, the sweet taste of fruit is irresistible for many animal species. As they roam around their environment, the animals feed on the fruit and pass out the seeds in their waste. This deposits the seeds in a new location and helps new plants spread out around their habitat. Other plants have different ways of dispersing their seeds. The fruits of some plants have evolved so that they can glide through the air themselves, without relying on animals to transport them. Some plants even have fruits that explode, scattering seeds across the ground as the fruit erupts. Once the seed has landed in the right spot, it's ready to begin sprouting as a new plant.

Flowers will eventually develop into fruits

"Turn the page to discover how different fruits help plants reproduce!"

Figs

Common fig trees have solid brown trunks and large floppy leaves. Hidden between the leaves are plump purple pods. These pods are the fig tree's fruit. If you tear one open, you can see a sticky mush inside. This mush used to be the fig tree's flowers. Fig trees need to spread their pollen around too. But if the flowers are hidden inside the fruit, how does the pollen reach them to create new seeds? Fig wasps burrow into fig fruits to lay their eggs. As they fly from fig to fig, the fig wasps bring the pollen with them. This fertilizes the fig's seeds, which then become ready to grow into new fig trees.

Sycamore seeds

Fruit grows in all shapes and sizes. In season, the winged fruits of maple and sycamore trees spin to the ground in their hundreds. These tall trees with patchy gray bark first evolved in Europe millions of years ago. Their seeds develop inside winged pods, which grow in bunches at the end of the tree's branches. When the time is right, the fruits drop off and flicker through the air on their wings. Once they have fallen onto fresh ground, they are ready to grow into new sycamore trees.

Peas

A pea pod is the fruit of a pea plant, and the peas inside are its seeds. If they aren't eaten by humans or other animals, the pea pod will split open when it becomes ripe. This throws the pea seeds out across its habitat. If they land in healthy soil, they might grow into new pea plants. Other plants also disperse their seeds in similar ways. When ripe, the so-called "exploding cucumber" bursts open with great intensity. The seeds inside can be fired out over many feet, to grow into new cucumber plants.

Durian

Sometimes fruits can be so offensive, some countries consider them against the law. The durian is a spiky fruit, large and heavy. It drops off the durian tree when ripe and splits open on the ground. In Southeast Asia where these fruits grow, people love the durian's unique taste. Some say it has the flavor of cheese-and-onion potato chips mixed with marzipan. But some find the strange smell so disgusting they choose to ban people from eating it in public places. Animals are free to eat the durian however and enjoy feasting on this stinky treat.

6. PLANT DISCOVERIES

ANCIENT FARMERS

"Thousands of years ago, ancient civilizations discovered that they did not have to go out into the wild and search for plants to eat—they could grow their own plants instead, much closer to home. These were the first farmers. They could use the plants they grew to feed their communities. A plant can be nutritious food, valuable material, or a useful source of fuel. Let's look more closely at the relationship between humans and plants . . ."

Plants and How to Grow Them

Around 10,000 years ago, human societies across the globe began to take seeds from the plants flourishing around them and grow them into new plants. First, they sowed the seeds in healthy soil. Then they looked after them, making sure they had enough light, water, and nutrients to sprout. In the Middle East, they grew grains such as wheat and barley. In South and Central America, they grew vegetables such as squashes and potatoes. These first farmers selected the best seeds from plants, and influenced the way new plants would grow. Corn was originally a wild grass. But through selecting the right seeds, ancient farmers turned it into the tasty corn we eat today.

Today, machines are used for farming.

The ancient cultures soon developed special techniques to grow plants faster than ever. In Sumeria, a region of the ancient Middle East, farmers understood that plants need water to grow. They developed a system to redirect water from nearby rivers into their fields.

Today, farmers grow a huge variety of plants from across the world. Potatoes and tomatoes are common ingredients in European and Asian cooking. But these plants were actually first grown by native societies in the Americas. Later, they were brought back to Europe by explorers.

Paper

Humans have always looked closely at the world around them. By studying it carefully they have discovered lots of new things. Writing has helped humans keep track of these discoveries. The Ancient Egyptians used plants for writing down important ideas. They dried out reeds that grew along the River Nile, and rubbed the plants into a pulp with stones. Then they flattened out the pulp to bake in the hot sun. When it had dried it would form a flat "papyrus" scroll to write on. These scrolls still exist today, helping historians learn more about Ancient Egypt.

Almost 2,000 years ago, a man in China invented a simpler way of recording ideas. Ts'ai Lun chopped up tree bark and mixed it with hemp-plant fibers and water. He flattened his mixture out, drained off the water, and let it dry. When Ts'ai Lun checked his concoction, it had turned into a pale flat sheet. He had invented paper! Ts'ai Lun's idea soon spread from China across the world.

ANCIENT WRITING

EXPLORER NOTES: *Plants have been used to make writing materials for millennia*

Ancient Egyptian papyrus

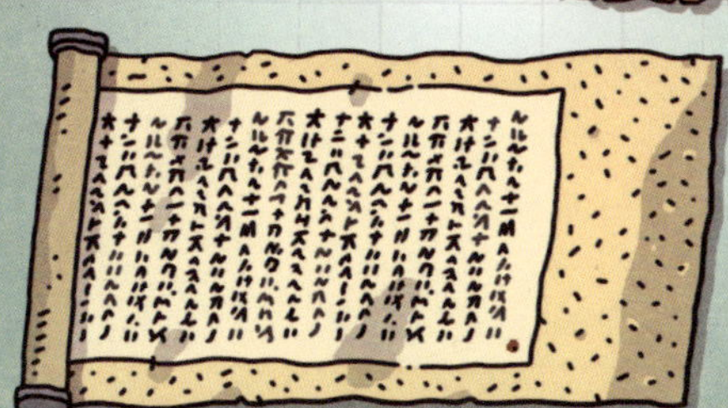

Ancient Chinese paper scroll

Coal powered many machines, including the first trains

Coal

In the Carboniferous period Earth was covered in plant life. Bushes, ferns, and trees grew everywhere. Over millions of years the forests died out. The remains of all the plants got squashed down beneath the soil. Deep underground they were transformed into "fossil fuels"—coal, gas, and oil. The plants' energy was trapped in these fuels for millions of years.

Today, humans dig or drill into the ground to find coal, gas, and oil. They burn what they dig up to release the energy trapped inside. Coal was the main source of power in the eighteenth and nineteenth-century Industrial Revolution in Europe. Factories and farms, boats and trains were all powered by coal-driven engines. Millions of people relied on the energy from the buried plants. Coal and gas are sources of energy humans still rely on today. Oil is used to make fuel and plastic. Using them produces pollution, but the modern world would be completely different without the energy these ancient plants provide.

"Turn the page to discover some of the greatest plant Explorers of all time!"

Who are the great plant Explorers?

Humans have always shared a close relationship with plants. They have made them into symbols in their cultures, religions, and art. They have turned them into unusual foods and used them to study the natural world around them. Here are my notes on some incredible people and the plants that inspired them.

THEOPHRASTUS | 371–287 BCE

EXPLORER NOTES: *Studied plants, their environment, and how they grew*

The Ancient Greeks paid close attention to the world around them, curious to know how everything worked. Scientist and thinker Aristotle explored and classified many animals. He recorded the creatures found in the Mediterranean region around Greece. But his friend Theophrastus was more interested in plants. He examined their leaves and saw how different species grew, checking the soil where their roots spread out. Amid the pines and the pomegranate trees, Theophrastus was one of the first ever "botanists," the scientific name for people who study plants.

LAKSHMI | Before 1000 BCE

EXPLORER NOTES: *Hindu goddess born from a lotus flower*

In perfect stillness on the surface of a pond, lotus flowers bloom in bright neon pink. Their golden pollen nestles in the center of their petals. Their stems are fastened to the bottom of the water by thick roots, while their green leaves float on the water's surface. The lotus is a symbol for purity and a clear mind in the Hindu religion, and is the sacred flower of the goddess Lakshmi, who stands for wealth, beauty, and good fortune.

MONTEZUMA | 1466–1520

EXPLORER NOTES: *Developed a taste for hot cocoa*

The Aztec Empire once stretched all over Mexico in Central America. From deep in the jungle, the Aztecs brought back beans from the cocoa plant. Cocoa was an Aztec delicacy. They turned the beans into a rich drink and added vanilla and cinnamon for flavor. The Aztec Emperor Montezuma was a cocoa addict. Legend says he drank fifty cups a day. When Europeans invaded Montezuma's territory, they took control of the cocoa and turned into cocoa guzzlers themselves. Hundreds of years later in eighteenth-century London, thousands of cafes served cocoa to their customers. Today, most cocoa beans are made into chocolate instead.

GREGOR MENDEL | 1822–1884

EXPLORER NOTES: *Studied inheritance through peas*

Gregor Mendel was a monk in eighteenth-century Austria. He wanted to understand how "inheritance" works—why brown-haired children might have "inherited" their parents' brown hair, or why a tall mother might have a daughter who is tall as well. But rather than investigate people, Mendel experimented with peas. In the gardens of his monastery, he tended to his pea plants. By mixing green peas and yellow peas, he discovered how parent plants pass on features to their offspring. He saw that the same patterns are at work in humans too. The lives of plants were teaching us about our own complex makeup.

MARIANNE NORTH | 1830–1890

EXPLORER NOTES: *Painted exotic plants from around the world*

Marianne North traveled the world and painted colorful illustrations of the plants that she saw. In Japan, she looked closely at the shapes of trees that grew on cold snowy mountains. In Jamaica, she studied the flowers that blossomed beside palm trees on the shore. She paid close attention to the details that others didn't notice. Kew Gardens in London have a special gallery dedicated to North and her images, a collection as extraordinary as the plants themselves.

LYNN MARGULIS | 1938–2011

EXPLORER NOTES: *Studied the origins of plant life*

This American biologist went right to the root of how plants actually work. She studied photosynthesis, the way plants use sunlight to produce the energy needed to survive. Margulis recognized how the first plants acquired this ability from organisms even older than the plants themselves—single-celled life-forms called "cyanobacteria." The first plants had absorbed the cyanobacteria into their cells. Once they had taken in these life-forms, the first plants also took on their unique ability to make energy out of the sun's light.

7. PLANTS AND HUMANS

DEFORESTATION

"The oldest plants first evolved millions of years ago. Over time, plants began to flourish in every climate across the globe. Other forms of life were evolving at the same time too. Different animals relied on plants for food and shelter. As humans developed, plants helped their societies grow. Earth would be an entirely different place without them. But how do humans and plants live together today? And how will they live together in the future?"

The Fate of the Forests

Thousands of years ago, humans began to grow plants themselves. At first they farmed these plants for food. Soon they found more uses for plants. They began making them into paper, clothes, or medicines. Later societies explored plants close-up. They investigated the way plants photosynthesize and affect the atmosphere. However, humans today are digging out the countryside and destroying forests on a bigger scale than ever before. As humans dig for fuel or cut down forests, they turn habitats upside down.

Forests and jungles are home to many animals

For life on Earth to stay secure, the gases in the atmosphere must remain at a stable level. If fewer plants are absorbing gases from the air for photosynthesis, Earth's atmosphere is pushed out of balance. Temperatures rise, contributing to a phenomenon called "global warming." Higher temperatures can have a damaging effect on living things on Earth. Many life-forms have not evolved to withstand these changes. For humans and all other species, a warmer Earth can mean more tornadoes, hurricanes, and other natural disasters. Homes and communities could be under threat. Today, human beings are beginning to understand they need to care for the environment and the plants and animals that live in it.

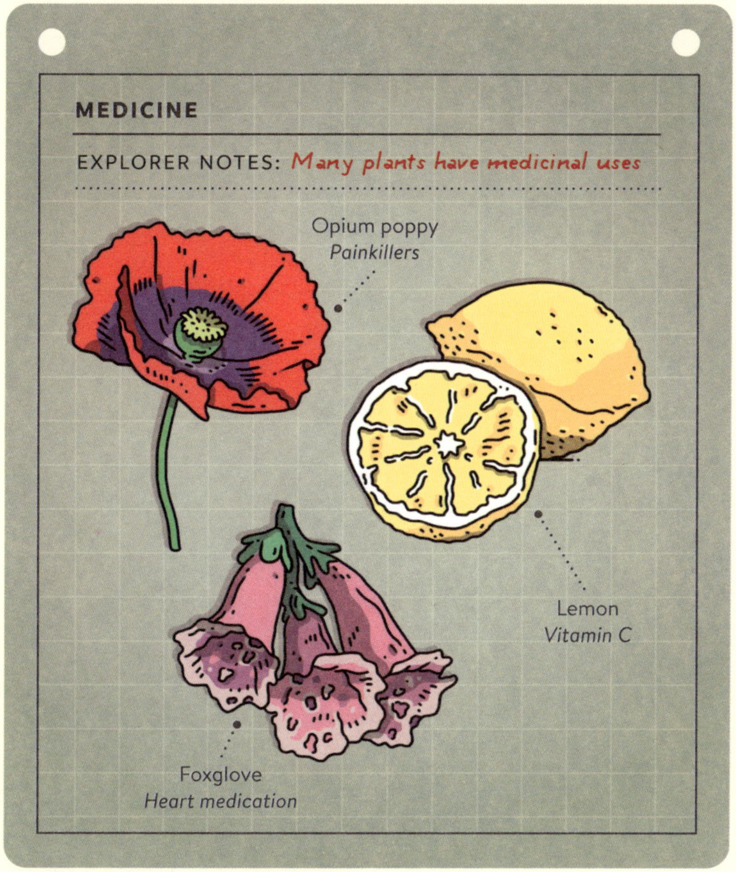

Plants and Medicine

Modern scientists invent medicines in laboratories. But in the past, people looked to the plants around them to find remedies for diseases. Sometimes these medicines could be helpful, such as a potion made from garlic for healing eye infections. But often these remedies were useless, such as using dandelions to cure sickness.

Over the centuries, better ways of using plants to keep healthy were discovered. Malaria is a vicious disease which kills thousands of people every year. But bark from the cinchona tree is proven to help malaria sufferers. Vitamin C is a substance found in citrus fruits such as lemons, limes, and oranges. It can help the body combat the common cold. Poppy plants can be used to create painkillers. Hospitals give these medicines to patients to help ease their symptoms. Foxglove flowers have even been used to make medicine for life-threatening heart conditions.

Science and Farming

Ancient farmers discovered that if they planted seeds from a plant that produced lots of fruit, the new plants would produce lots of fruit too. The older plants contained the right "genes" to make lots of fruit grow. Genes are codes found in the cells of each living thing that instruct the cells how to grow. Older plants pass these genes on to the new plants in their seeds. Modern scientists are trying to achieve the same results as the ancient farmers. But today they can change a plant's genes in a laboratory. Some believe this method will help produce plants that will always be healthy and crops that produce extra fruits or nutrients. Other people are not sure if this method is safe, or that it really can help to end world hunger. But the scientists continue to experiment. Humans are always looking for new ways of farming plants to help feed a growing global population.

Scientists have developed rice containing extra nutrients

"Turn the page to discover how some more incredible uses for plants!"

Rubber

Rubber trees originally came from the humid jungles of the Americas, but have been taken across the globe by humans. They have tall, sturdy trunks and round leaves. Humans tap into their bark to draw out a milky liquid from the trunk. Then they turn the liquid into rubber. This stretchy substance can be used for making many things. Humans use rubber to make car tires, rubber gloves, tennis balls, boots, even underwater diving equipment. The plant is so important that in the seventeenth century, Europeans set up a secret network to smuggle the trees out of Brazil and get them to Europe. The Brazilians tried to ban these undercover operations, but some seeds got through. Soon people in England could see tropical rubber trees growing in Kew Gardens in London.

Sugar

Humans have farmed sugar plants for hundreds of years. Ancient Greeks called the dried sugar they first came across in India "honey powder." Modern societies continue to enjoy sugar's sweet taste. Sugar crystals are made from the sweet liquid inside the thick stalks of sugarcane, a giant grass. Harvesting sugar is hard work. From around the sixteenth century, Europeans took people from Africa and the Americas and forced them to perform this work as slaves. For hundreds of years, they kept them on their farms in brutal conditions.

Tea

Ancient legends say that making tea from the leaves of the tea plant first began in China thousands of years ago. Although tea historians are not sure of the date, records do suggest China is the true home of tea. Around 200 BCE, whether emperor or rice farmer, all kinds of Chinese people began to enjoy a hot cup of tea. Its popularity quickly spread to Japan, Korea and India. The thin green leaves growing on tea plants are plucked, dried, and then boiled to make a cup of this satisfying drink.

Cotton

There are dozens of species of cotton plants. They thrive all over the world—from America to China, from India to Brazil. The wispy threads that grow around cotton seeds can be woven into fabric to make clothes. The earliest civilizations to make cotton clothes developed in India and Pakistan. Later, societies in the West relied on slave labor to pick the cotton. They transported millions of people from Africa to work as slaves on plantations in distant lands.

AGENT OSPREY'S PLANT PUZZLERS

We've explored the whole history of how plants developed on Earth—from ancient algae floating in the sea, to the trees, bushes, and flowers growing all over the world today. Now it's time to see if you've been paying attention! Let's run through some questions to check we've got our facts straight ...

WHAT'S THAT FRUIT?

My field notes and sketches have got muddled up in my Explorer rucksack and now they're all over the place. Can you help match the right description to the right fruit?

A. When this fruit is ripe, it bursts and scatters its seeds all around

B. Spinning through the air on slim wings, this is the fruit of a tall tree

C. A fruit with such a strong smell, it's restricted by local authorities

1. DURIAN

2. SYCAMORE

3. OAK

4. CHILI PEPPER

5. PEAS

6. FIG

THE PLANT QUIZ

Read my report carefully to discover the answers.

1. WHAT ARE PLANTS?
Which three ingredients are essential for plants to photosynthesize?

a) Water, air, and sunlight
b) Sugar, flowers, and minerals
c) Algae, leaves, and bark

2. PLANT ORIGINS
The earliest plants didn't rely on seeds for reproduction. What were the small clusters of cells they used instead, still found on many plants today?

a) Eggs cells
b) Fruits
c) Spores

3. PLANT PLANET
What problems did plants face from the extra oxygen they produced in the Carboniferous period?

a) The extra oxygen meant more wildfires, wiping out entire forests
b) The oxygen caused the growth of giant insects which ate up all their leaves
c) The extra oxygen influenced the spread of a tree-eating disease

4. SURVIVAL SECRETS
What trick do cycads use to get insects to visit them?

a) They can attract insects by raising their cones' temperatures
b) They emit a low droning sound to attract passing bugs
c) Their leaves are covered in sticky sugar, which insects eat

5. FRUITS AND FLOWERS
Why do insects visit flowers?

a) To drink the sweet nectar within the flower's petals
b) To pick up the flower's scent and attract other insects
c) To find a safe warm place to lay their eggs

6. PLANT DISCOVERIES
Why did the Austrian monk Gregor Mendel grow pea plants at his monastery?

a) To attract colorful birds which ate the peas
b) To learn how pea plants inherit characteristics from their parents' seeds
c) To sell to the local villagers at the vegetable market

7. PLANTS AND HUMANS
In the Middle Ages, what magical healing powers did people associate with garlic?

a) It stopped you turning into a vampire
b) It could cure eye problems
c) It could stop you being infected by the Plague

CLUB NOTICES

GLOSSARY

EAGLE EYED APPROVED

ADAPTATION
Any special feature an organism has is an adaptation—huge leaves, a thick trunk, or colorful flowers. Adaptations can be passed on to the next generation, and can help organisms to survive.

ALGAE
Photosynthesizing organisms which are the ancestors of plants. Algae develop in many forms, from single cells to giant seaweeds.

CHLOROPLASTS
Tiny structures in plant cells where photosynthesis takes place. Chloroplasts contain the chemical chlorophyll, which is green and gives plants their color.

CONIFERS
Plants with seeds which develop inside a cone. Conifers are widespread in colder climates. Some of the tallest plants in the world are conifer trees.

DOMESTICATION
The process of changing organisms so they are more useful for humans. This could mean developing plants which grow more fruit, or survive in harsher environments, for example.

FOSSILS
Traces left behind by long-dead organisms, including plants. Fossils tell scientists about organisms which lived millions of years ago.

FOSSIL FUELS
Substances produced by dead plants being squashed down over millions of years, conserving their energy. Humans rely on fossil fuels for many things, including energy, but using them is also polluting.

HABITAT
The environment an organism is adapted to and lives in. Plants' habitats can be dry deserts or fast-flowing rivers. Plants also form habitats for other creatures, such as birds.

PHOTOSYNTHESIS
A process for making energy from sunlight, carbon dioxide gas, and water. Plants rely on photosynthesis for the energy to survive.

POLLINATION
A form of sexual reproduction found in many plants. Pollen from a male plant mixes with ova from a female one and these form into a seed, ready to grow into a new plant.

SPORES
Reproductive cells produced by many plants, and fungi too. Spores do not have a thick outer-coating like seeds or as large a store of nutrients, water, and energy for the new plant.

VASCULAR PLANTS
Plants with tubes through their bodies which are used to transport water and gases. Most plants today are vascular plants.

THE TEAM

NICK FORSHAW
Nick is a writer based in Berlin. He holds a BA and MA in film and literary studies. He hopes his readers love learning about the world and all the things in it just as much as he does.

WILLIAM EXLEY
William is an illustrator living in Southeast London. When not illustrating Explorer books he also works on comics. Will's favorite plant is the coffee plant.

AQUILA NON CAPIT MUSCAS
THE EAGLE DOES NOT CATCH FLIES

MISSION 01

DINOSAURS!

MISSION 02
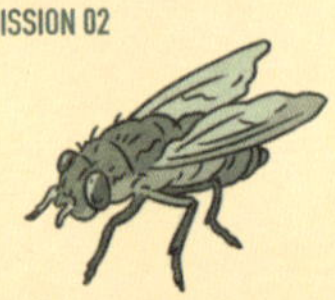
BUGS!

MISSION 03
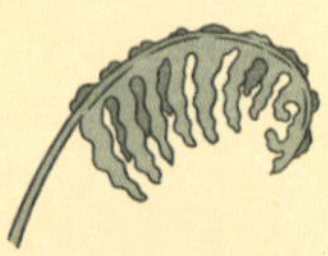
PLANTS!

MISSION 04

MAMMALS!

EXPLORER MISSIONS
Find out more at whatonearthbooks.com

Entries in *italic* can be found in the Timeline.

THE PLANT TIMELINE

We've made it back to the library! Time to look over our findings. Unfold the epic Timeline that traces the entire history of plant life, showcasing 100 different species. Can you find a fruit which floats on water? A giant grass which grows almost 3 feet per day? Or a poisonous plant which caused the death of an ancient philosopher?

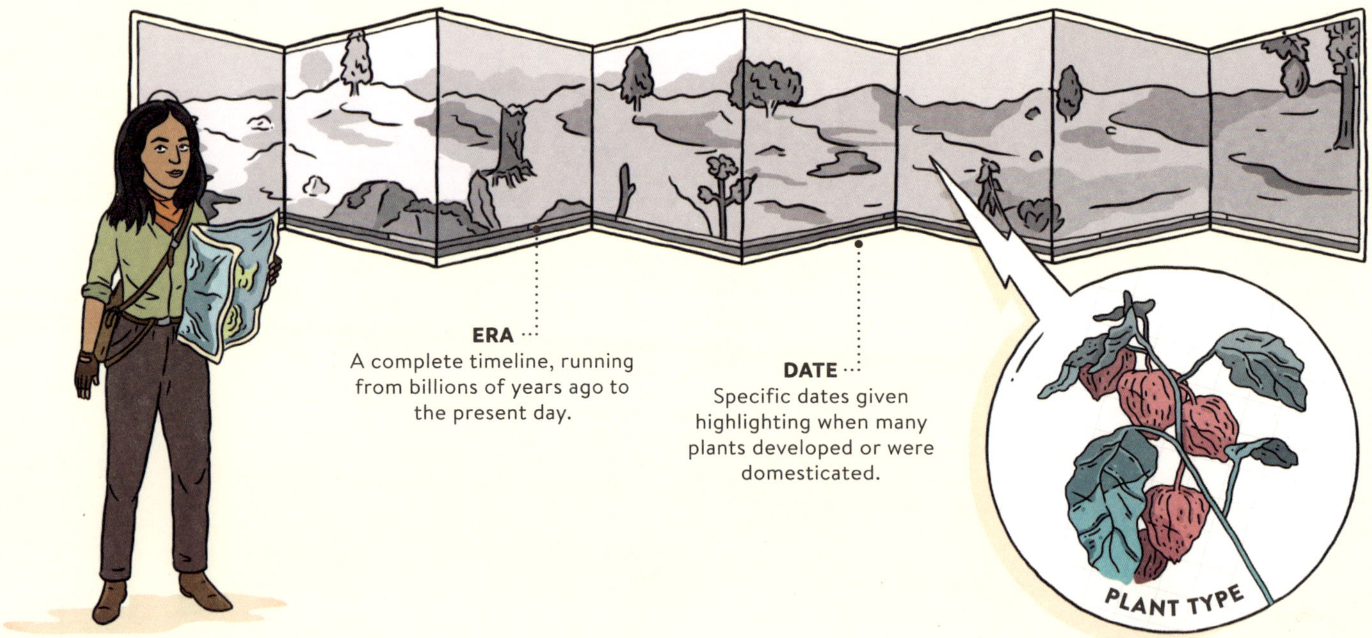

EXPLORER

PLANTS!

CYANOBACTERIA
These organisms consist of only single cells, or chains of cells. They were among the first to develop the system called "photosynthesis," taking in sunlight to store energy. The chlorophyll chemical involved gives plants their green color.

CARYOSPHEROIDES
Simple plants which lived in water, these were some of the first green algae. Similar forms are still found in oceans, seas, rivers, and lakes today.

PRIMICORALLINA
The stem and branches of this ancient alga were made up of just a single huge cell.

PALEONITELLA
Close relatives of the first plants to develop on land. The strong structures in the cell walls of this alga later provided extra support for these plants on dry land.

RHYNIE CHERT PLANTS
All these plants were discovered in the Rhynie Chert, a single fossil site in Scotland from 410 million years ago, which provides a unique glimpse into the lives of ancient organisms.

COOKSONIA
One of the first plants to grow on dry land. This new environment brought new challenges, so *Cooksonia* developed internal tubes for transporting water from the soil to its branches.

AGLAOPHYTON
This land plant's branches ended in special organs which produced "spores," cells which grow into new plants.

RHYNIA
Specialized cells on this plant anchored it in the soil and absorbed water. Rhynia relied on tiny fungi below the ground to scavenge extra nutrients from the soil.

EOPHYLLOPHYTON
One of the first plants to develop a revolutionary feature—basic leaves only a ⅛ inch long grew from its branches. These produced the energy needed to survive, through photosynthesis.

ASTEROXYLON
The stem of this plant was covered in scale-like leaves. Surface pores called "stomata" allowed gases to flow to and from the air.

HORNEOPHYTON
The stem of this plant contained hollow tubes for transferring water up from the soil. Below ground, the end of the stem was covered in hair-like cells, which absorbed water and anchored it in the soil.

SCIADOPHYTON
The branches of this plant grew outwards and upwards from its center, like points on a star. Each ended in a bowl-shaped structure where reproductive cells mixed to begin the next stage in the plant's life cycle.

DREPANOPHYCUS
The tiny spines which covered this plant were actually leaves. *Drepanophycus* was a simple but successful plant—a "club moss"—found today on mountains and in forests.

EOSPERMATOPTERIS
An early tree which grew to around 26ft-tall. Its thick trunk kept it stable while it reached above other plants for better access to sunlight.

CALAMOPHYTON
One of the first trees. The top of this 13ft-tall plant developed a crown of leaves that were shed as the plant grew.

PSILOPHYTON
A distant ancestor of ferns and of seed-producing plants, two groups which include most plant species today.

RUNCARIA
A special coating partly surrounded *Runcaria's* reproductive cells. These enclosed cells were some of the first seeds.

CLADOXYLON
Between the branches of this plant was a thin "webbing." In later relatives, it completely filled the gaps between branches, developing into the broad leaves that most plants have today.

ARCHEOPTERIS
These 33ft tall trees had woody trunks and leaves like ferns. Their unusual combination of features isn't found in any plants alive today. *Archeopteris* had extra pores on its surface to better absorb the lower levels of gases in the air at the time.

RHACOPHYTON
With leaf-like branches, this plant was an ancestor of ferns. Fossils of *Rhacopyhton* show some of the earliest signs of wildfires that destroyed large areas of plant life in a flash.

HEPATICITES
These plants were related to liverworts. Without special structures for transferring water, liverworts grow in moist environments where water is plentiful anyway.

ALLOIOPTERIS
As these plants died and decomposed, they were compressed and transformed over millions of years into rocky coal, used today as fuel. They were probably related to ferns.

MORESNETIA
One of the earliest known plants to develop seeds. Sealed in their case, these early seeds could store nutrients and water for the developing plant, allowing it to wait for the best growing conditions.

SIGILLARIA
This 66ft-tall tree was crowned with spiraling leaves and lived near rivers. As the tree grew, the old leaves fell off, but left behind a pattern of scars on the trunk that can be seen in fossils.

ARCHEOCALAMITES
These plants were related to ferns but had leaves like small hairs, giving them the name "horsetails." Although rare today, they were common in the swamps of the Carboniferous.

LEPIDODENDRON
Fossils of this 130ft-tall plant have been discovere across the globe, showing was widespread during th Carboniferous. Its scaly t was green and soft, unlik hard bark of today's trees

MEDU
With b 23ft-lo like fer they d reprod Scienti ferns. group

MUSCITES
One of the first mos plants which can be shady spots with lots often forming a carp fallen trees and fore

ECAMBRIAN PERIOD	CAMBRIAN, ORDOVICIAN, AND SILURIAN PERIODS		DEVONIAN PERIOD		CARBONIFEROUS PERIOD	
1000 Mya (Million years ago)	500 Mya	400 Mya		370 Mya	340 Mya	310 My

Pineapple

Sacred lotus

WALCHIA
One of the first conifers – trees with seeds protected inside a cone. Its branches were covered in tiny needle-like leaves. Conifers dominated forests for over 150 million years.

NIUS
n was huge like it grew to 33ft leaves up to g. The branching f ferns are s "fronds."

up to s looked erns, to spores. seed ecial

INSECTS
Damage from chewing insects and other animals can be seen on many plant fossils and can reveal clues about the diets of ancient animals.

PSEUDOMARIOPTERIS
This seed fern used other plants for support as it climbed. Climbers have special adaptations for clinging onto plants and rocks, such as hooks, barbs, or sticky pads.

CORDAITES
Although this tree's seeds developed inside cones, it wasn't a conifer. It mostly liked swampy ground, and some of the examples reached 150ft-tall.

OTOVICIA
The environment became hotter and drier during *Otovicia*'s time. While species that needed lots of water suffered, these conifers found success.

GLOSSOPTERIS
Fossils of this seed fern have been found in South America, Africa, India, Australia, and even Antarctica. These continents were joined together into a single supercontinent called Gondwana at the time.

LEPIDOPTERIS
Fossils show the number of "stomata," special pores on *Lepidopteris*'s surface, changed over time, suggesting the atmosphere and climate were changing. Indeed, soon after 252 million years ago, many species died in a mass extinction.

VOLTZIA
Huge forests of these conifers stretched along the coastline, away from the drier conditions farther inland.

ARAUCARIOXYLON
Huge forests of this 200ft-tall conifer were fossilized in Arizona. Later, local people constructed homes from the stone-like (petrified) wood.

DICROIDIUM
This seed fern was "deciduous," meaning it lost its leaves as the seasons changed. This adaptation helped it conserve water in dry periods.

LEPTOCYCAS
Although they looked like palm trees, these plants developed their own group, the cycads. Once widespread, cycads would have provided plentiful food for hungry dinosaurs.

AGATHOXYLON
Some of the fossil wood of this conifer was transformed over millions of years into "jet," a black gemstone prized for use in jewelry.

WILLIAMSONIA
These 6½ft-tall plants were common in the Triassic and Jurassic periods and would have been a major part of the diet of many dinosaurs.

GINKGO
These trees are true survivors—a single species held on until today. They are known for their beautiful fan-shaped leaves, as well as the stink of their large seeds.

ANDROSTROBUS
This cycad is only known from its woody cones. Male cones contain pollen, while female cones contain ovules. When pollen and ovule mix, a seed forms.

ARCHEFRUCTUS
One of the first flowering plants, its name means "ancient fruit." *Archefructus* fossils show that one species had separate male and female flowers, while another combined the two into a single flower.

ALVINIA
This tree was pollinated by bugs with specially adapted mouthparts for extracting its pollen. The bugs would take the pollen from plant to plant, helping *Alvinia* to reproduce.

ARCHEANTHUS
These flowering plants developed clusters of seed-filled fruits, which have been preserved as fossils.

BAIERA
This tree was a relative of ginkgoes. Although its group was once diverse and widespread, today only a single species remains.

MONTSECHIA
This early flowering plant grew in freshwater lakes. It probably developed from an earlier flowering land-plant that had adapted to water.

PERMIAN PERIOD
TRIASSIC PERIOD
JURASSIC PERIOD
CRETACEOUS PERIOD

280 Mya
250 Mya
220 Mya
190 Mya
160 Mya
130 Mya
100 Mya

Fig tree

Maple tree

CALYPTUS
est fires are usually a
eat for plants, but this
e would spring back to
after fire, thriving on
extra nutrients in the
l from burnt plants.

K-T EXTINCTION
After the impact of an enormous meteor, a changing climate saw many plants and animals become extinct. Flowering plants quickly filled the gap left by other species, going on to dominate the world today.

tree, fig trees are pollinated by a
p which lays their eggs inside its
flowers. These flowers eventually
we call the fig's fruit, although it
luster of fruits, each containing a
elationship between fig and wasp
for the tree's survival.

AGNOLIA
e reproductive parts of this
ant's flowers were arranged
a spiral. In many plants
day, they are arranged in
ring instead, but magnolias
till show this older system.

ASOS
s of this plant
rved in amber
roduction. Tiny
ns can be seen
rough the flower
the egg cell and
lly become a seed.

COCONUT
The hard exterior of a coconut palm's fruits enclose the familiar hairy middle layer. Coconuts float long distances on the world's oceans before growing into new plants.

PHYSALIS
Remarkably, the fossilized fruit of this plant was discovered intact. Some plants in its group today produce deadly poisons, but others are safe to eat such as tomatoes, potatoes, and eggplants.

MANGROVE
These trees grew in water. Their special roots filtered out toxic salt from seawater and took in extra nutrients from the soggy soil. Today, mangroves form thick forests along coastlines around the world.

PINE
These conifer trees are common today in colder climates. But flowering plants became the most successful group during this period, pushing out other types such as these conifers.

METASEQUOIA
These conifers lived in forests in the north of Canada, when the Earth was warmer. Their fossils have even been found under layers of ice inside the frozen Arctic Circle.

RORIDULA
This plant had sticky-haired leaves for trapping bugs, but it wasn't a meat-eater—it took nutrients from the droppings of animals that came to eat the trapped bugs.

GRAMINIDITES
The flower heads of this plant were made up of hundreds of individual tiny flowers. Its relatives today, including sunflowers and daisies, have the same "composite" flowers.

OAK
This tree developed long clusters of flowers called catkins, which hung from its branches and have been preserved as fossils. Wind blew the pollen from tree to tree for reproduction.

PROTEA
These plants had eye-catching flower heads, which were really clusters of smaller flowers. Proteas flourish today in warm, dry conditions across the southern hsemisphere.

STRYCHNOS
The tiny flowers of this plant were found preserved in amber. Plants from its group produce the poison strychnine, which protects the plant from being eaten by animals.

CACTUS
The spines of cactuses retain water to adapt to the desert conditions. Cactuses quickly absorb extra water when rain falls and develop juicy fruits, despite their dry environment.

TURKISH PINE
A forest of these conifers was fossilized on the Greek island of Lesbos by falling ash from a volcanic eruption. The remains of the trees have formed hard stones dotted across the landscape.

MAPLE
The cases around the seeds of these trees were structured like pairs of wings. As they spiraled down, they were carried away on the wind, dispersing the seeds.

MELLIORCHIS
This orchid is only known from its pollen, which was found attached to a bee preserved in amber. Orchids are some of the most diverse plants, and are well-known for their stunning flowers.

SUGARCANE
This grass has a stem full of sugar! People living on New Guinea began eating the wild sugarcane long ago. Today, the plants are usually boiled and refined to produce sugar.

BARLEY
This grass was one of the first plants grown by humans when they settled in one place and abandoned their roaming lifestyles over 10,000 years ago. Humans bred plants to produce larger grains and to survive harsher conditions.

BRISTLECONE PINE
These plants can survive for over 5,000 years, making them the oldest living organisms in the world. Today, scientists study the rings inside their trunks for clues to the planet's history.

TOBACCO
Local people from the Andes chewed the leaves of this plant because of the addictive chemical nicotine they contained. Today, smoking tobacco is responsible for hundreds of millions of deaths every year.

FARMING
Around 10,000 years ago, people began growing plants themselves for food. Farming has allowed human societies to support much bigger populations ever since.

CHILI PEPPER
The fruits of this plant produce a chemical which causes a painfully hot sensation when eaten. People in ancient Peru and Ecuador developed a taste for their spicy kick.

GRAPE VINES
Ancient peoples across the Mediterranean fermented grapes to create wine, originally as medicine. Grapes are found naturally covered in fermenting yeast, which may have led to the discovery of wine.

TEA PLANT
Legend holds that C
Emperor Shennong
discovered tea whe
accidentally fell int
water, and he enjoy
invigorating drink.

HEMP
For thousands
hemp's strong
been used for
cloth. But tod
and consumin
illegal in many

COTTON
The white fibe
develop aroun
this plant catc
of passing ani
to disperse its
Humans use th
spin into threa

PALEOGENE PERIOD | NEOGENE PERIOD

70 Mya | 50 Mya | 40 Mya | 30 Mya | 20 Mya | 10 Mya | 0 Mya | 5000 BCE | 2500 BCE

Glossopteris

Androstrobus

CACAO
The seeds of this tree are used to produce chocolate. Cocoa "beans" were first used in Central America to produce a bitter drink, later sweetened with sugar by the Europeans.
COFFEE
This seeds of this plant contain caffeine. Legend has it that an Ethiopian goatherd discovered it when his goats behaved strangely after eating coffee seeds. Today, 500 billion cups of coffee are drunk annually.
PINEAPPLE
The unusual fruits of these plants were presented to rulers across Europe by explorers returning from South America. At one banquet organized by English King Charles II, a pineapple took center stage.
CITRUS
The fruits of thee plants, which include oanges, lemons, and limes, contan Vitamin C. They were packd on ships for long sea-voyges for their health benefits,where diseases such as scurvy vere common.
BANANA
Worldwide banana stocks were nearly decimated in 1950 when a fungus wiped out the most popular variety. Originally grown in Indonesia and considered unusual, bananas are now an everyday snack across the globe.
COAST REDWOOD
These conifers are the tallest organisms on Earth, dwarfing other plants and animals. The tallest known example, Hyperion, stands 380ft-tall (the height of 70 people!).
RUBBER TREE
Rubber, made from the fluid of some plants, was first harvested in Central America to make balls for sport. Since then, rubber has been used to make waterproof clothes and machinery, among other things.
HEMLOCK
This plant's poison causes paralysis and even death. It was used in Ancient Greece for the ultimate punishment—the philosopher Socrates was executed with hemlock because of his revolutionary beliefs.
GARLIC
Medieval doctors recommended a mixture of garlic, wine, and bull's bile as a cure for eye infections. Garlic is more commonly used today in cooking.
PEA PLANT
Peasnight be on your dinnr plate tonight, but Austian monk Gregor Menel studied different genetions of these plants and iscovered the basics of gnetics.
OIL PALM
Huge plantations have sprung up across the Indian Ocean and South America to produce vegetable oil from these plants' fruits, but this has endangered rain forests in the process.
DURIAN
Durian fruit has such a terrible smell that it is banned on public transport in Singapore. To some, it tastes of cheese, onions, and almonds, but others consider it a delicacy.
RAFFLESIA
This plant has the largest flower in the world, with some growing to 3ft in diameter. The flowers produce a disgusting rotting-meat smell to attract flies and beetles, which pollinate the plant.
OPIUM POPPY
The addictive drug opium is produced from this plant. Trading in opium caused wars between Britain and China with British traders attempting to profit from China's addiction.
CINCHONA
The bark of this tree contains the chemical quinine, which protects against the disease malaria. The recipe for the first tonic was developed by Christian priests who often traveled the world to regions affected by the disease.
TWINFLOWER
This small forest flower was a favorite of Swedish botanist Carl Linnaeus, who developed the *Systema Naturae*, the basis of the modern system for classifying living things.
ROSE
This thorny plant has been bred to produce flowers of many colors. In medieval England, white and red roses were the symbols of the rival Yorkist and Lancastrian families during the Wars of the Roses.
ANT-HOUSE PLANT
These plants contain structures called "domatia" which ants build as secure homes inside the plant's stem. But, far from being a nuisance, the resident ants guard their new home from plant-eaters and vines.
BAMBOO
Bamboo is actually a giant grass and the fastest growing plant in the world. It can grow 3ft per day, and the largest species can reach more than 100ft in height.
RICE
The tiny seeds of this plant are a staple food for billions of people across the globe. Scientists have created Golden Rice with extra Vitamin A through genetic engineering.
SACRED LOTUS
Lotuses grow from the bottom of lakes and rivers to produce a stunning flower which is held above the water's surface. In the Hindu religion, the god Brahma is said to have been born from a lotus flower.
MAIZE
This grass was bred by Central Americans to produce bigger fruit, resulting in the familiar corncob. One Central American creation story described how humans were made from corn by the gods.
TULIP
During the 1630s, the Netherlands was overcome with "tulip mania." Single tulip bulbs sold for huge amounts of money. The trade collapsed overnight, and tulip merchants went out of business.
POTATO
Potatoes originated in the mountains of South America. In Ireland in 1845, a disease affecting potatoes caused almost one million people to die and another one million to emigrate when famine struck.
VENUS FLYTRAP
When a bug touches the trap, this meat-eating plant closes up and the bug is digested. Charles Darwin called it "one of the most wonderful plants in the world."
QUATERNARY PERIOD
0 CE
1000 CE
1500 CE
1750 CE
2000 CE
Present day

Sciadophyton

Archeopteris